HILLROCKS COLORING BOOK

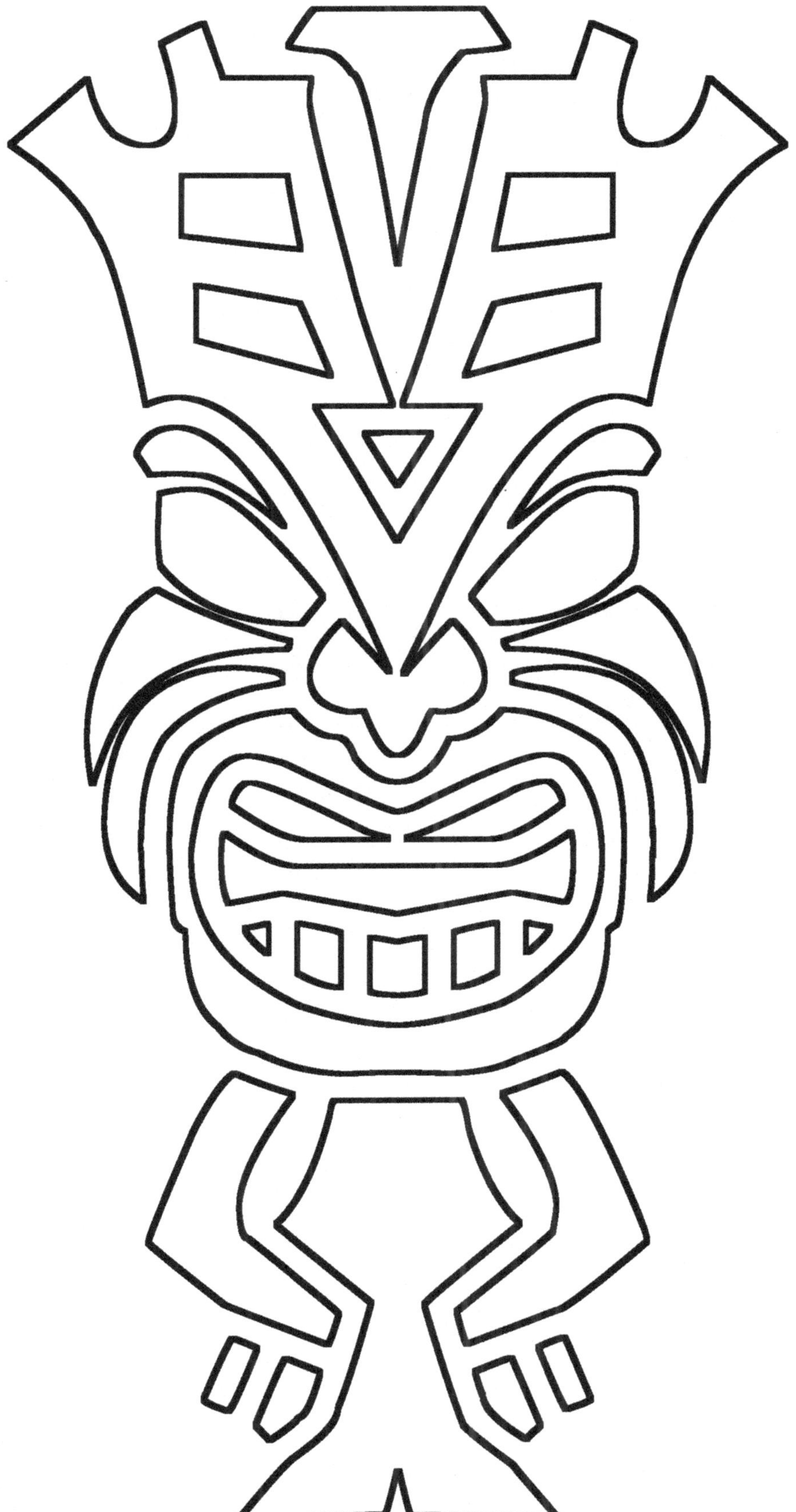

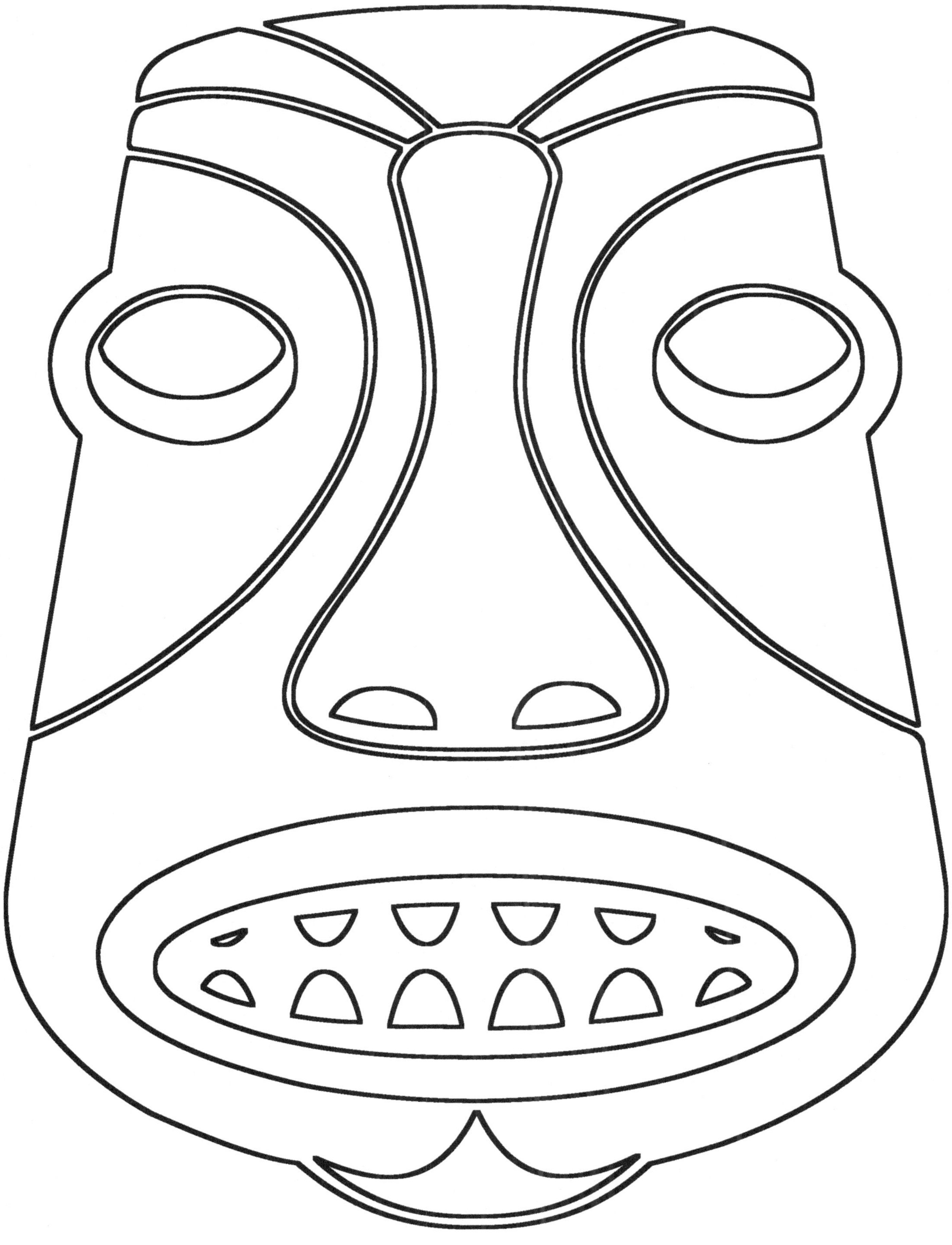

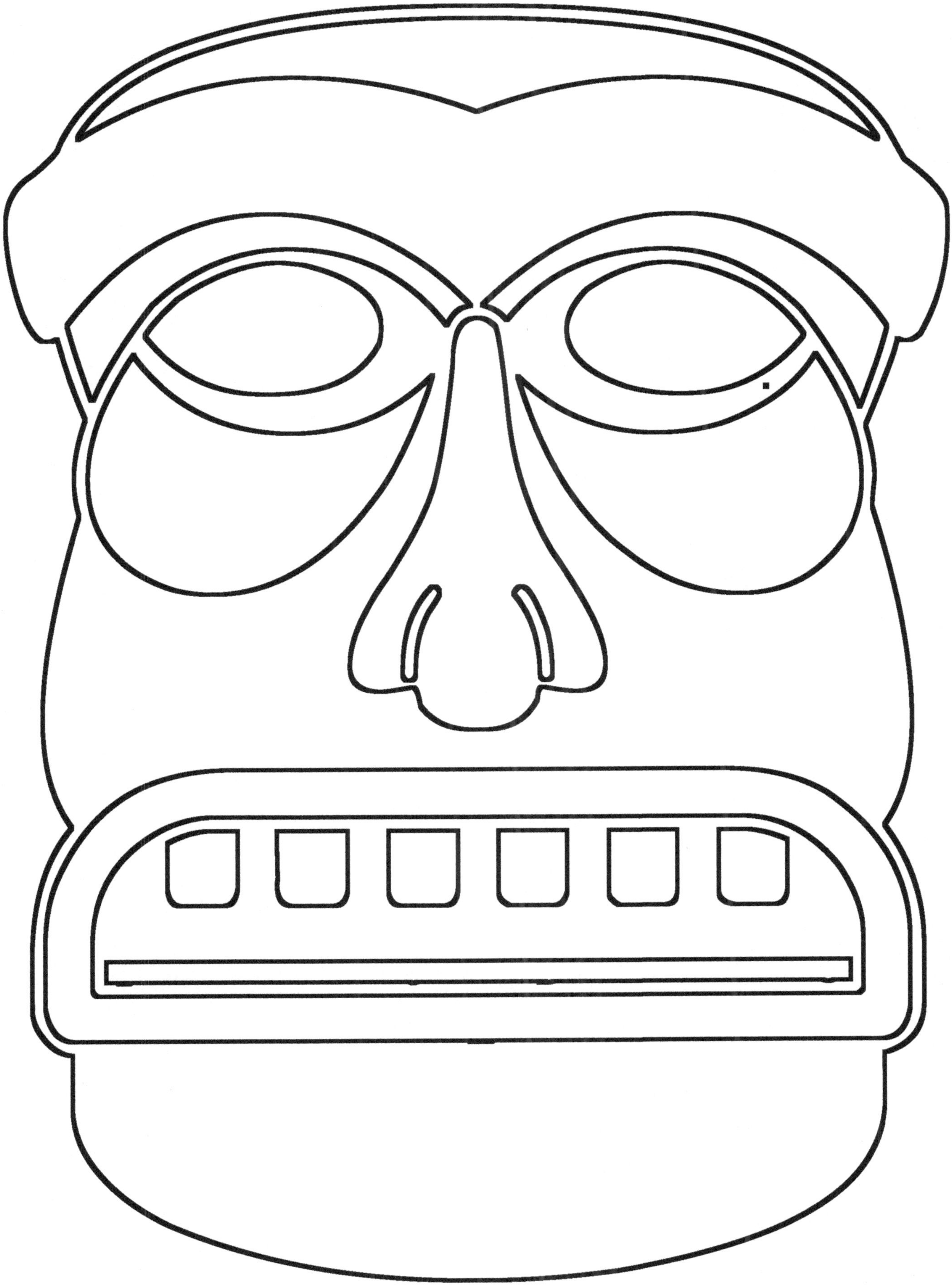

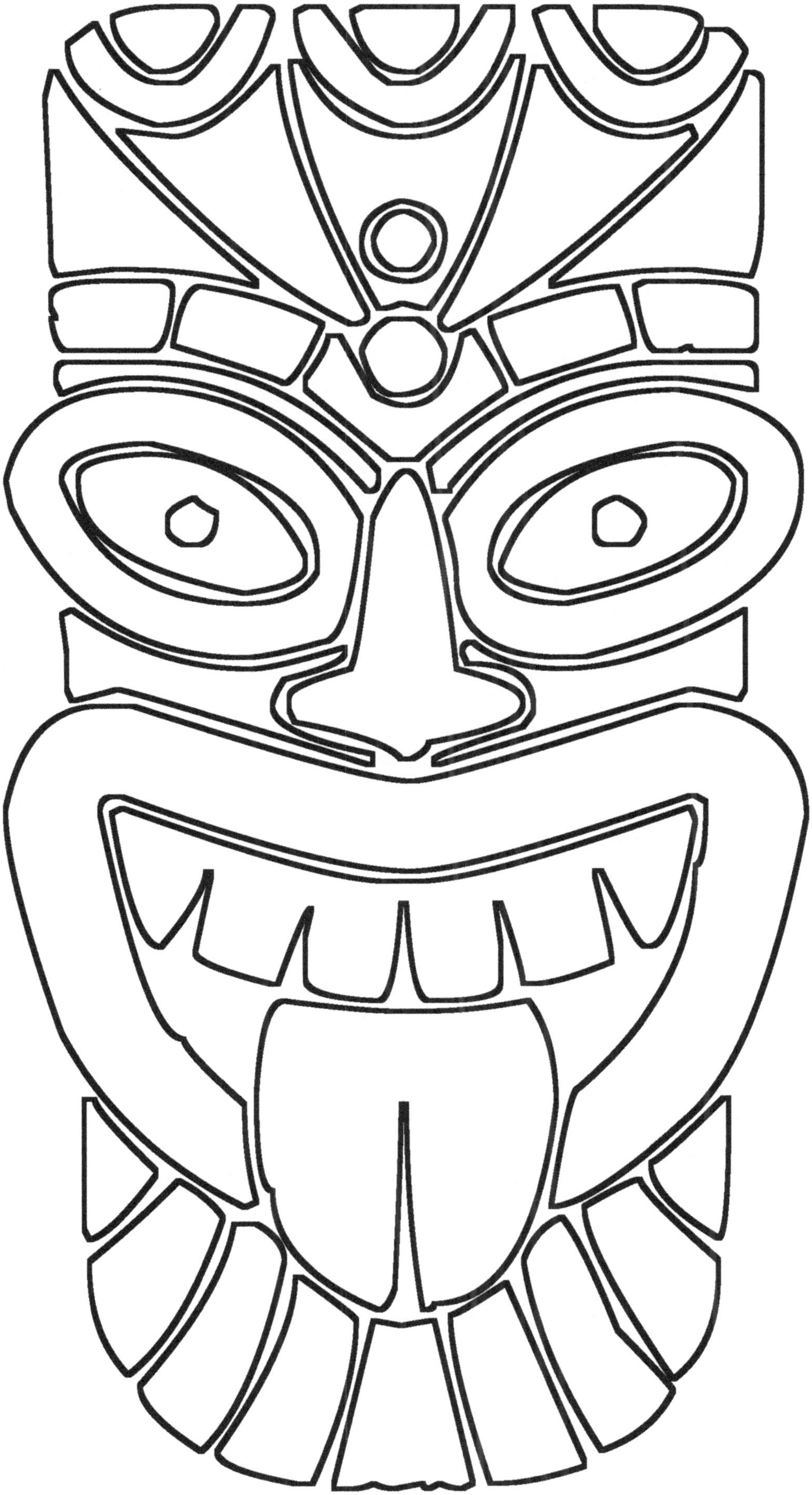

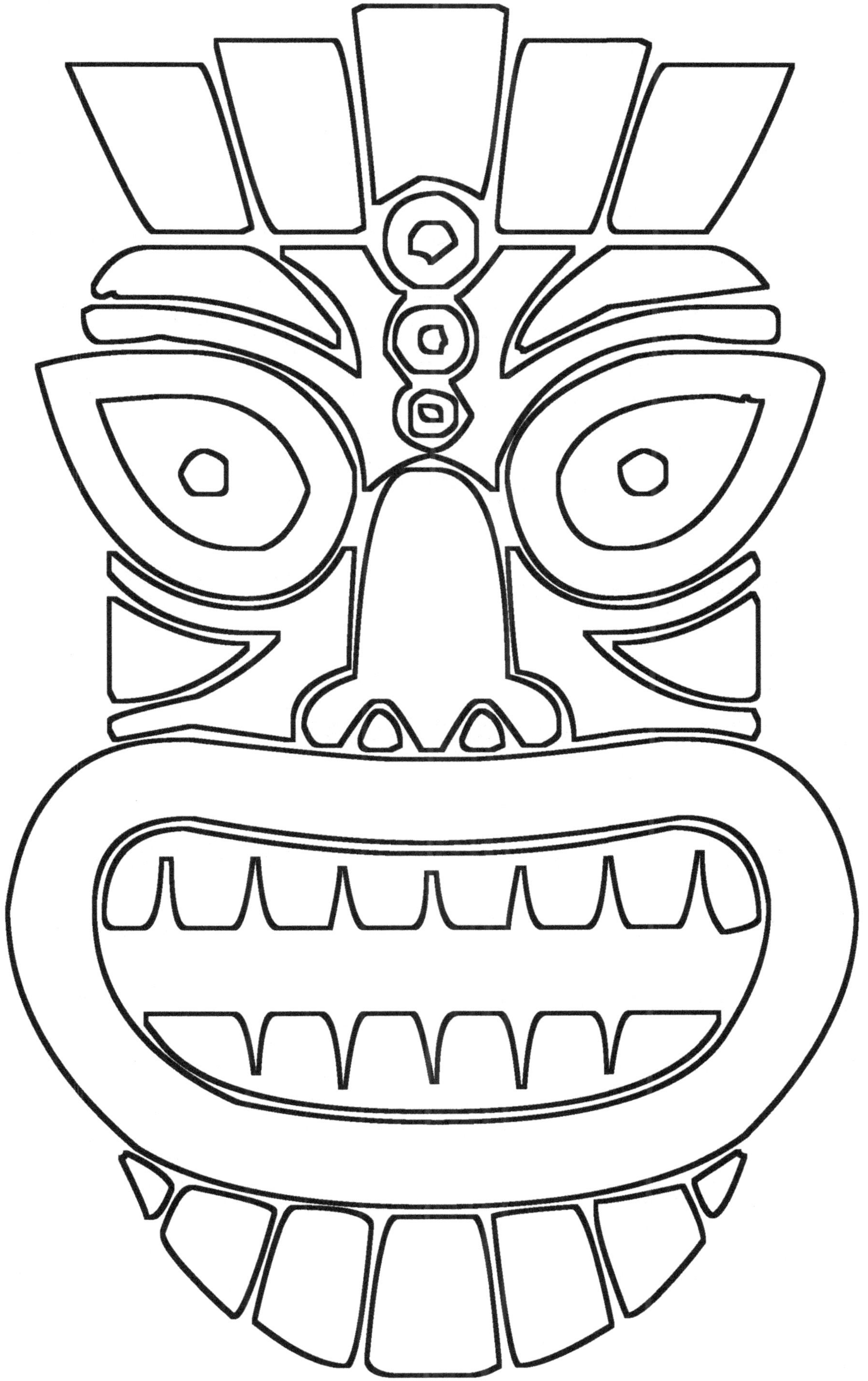

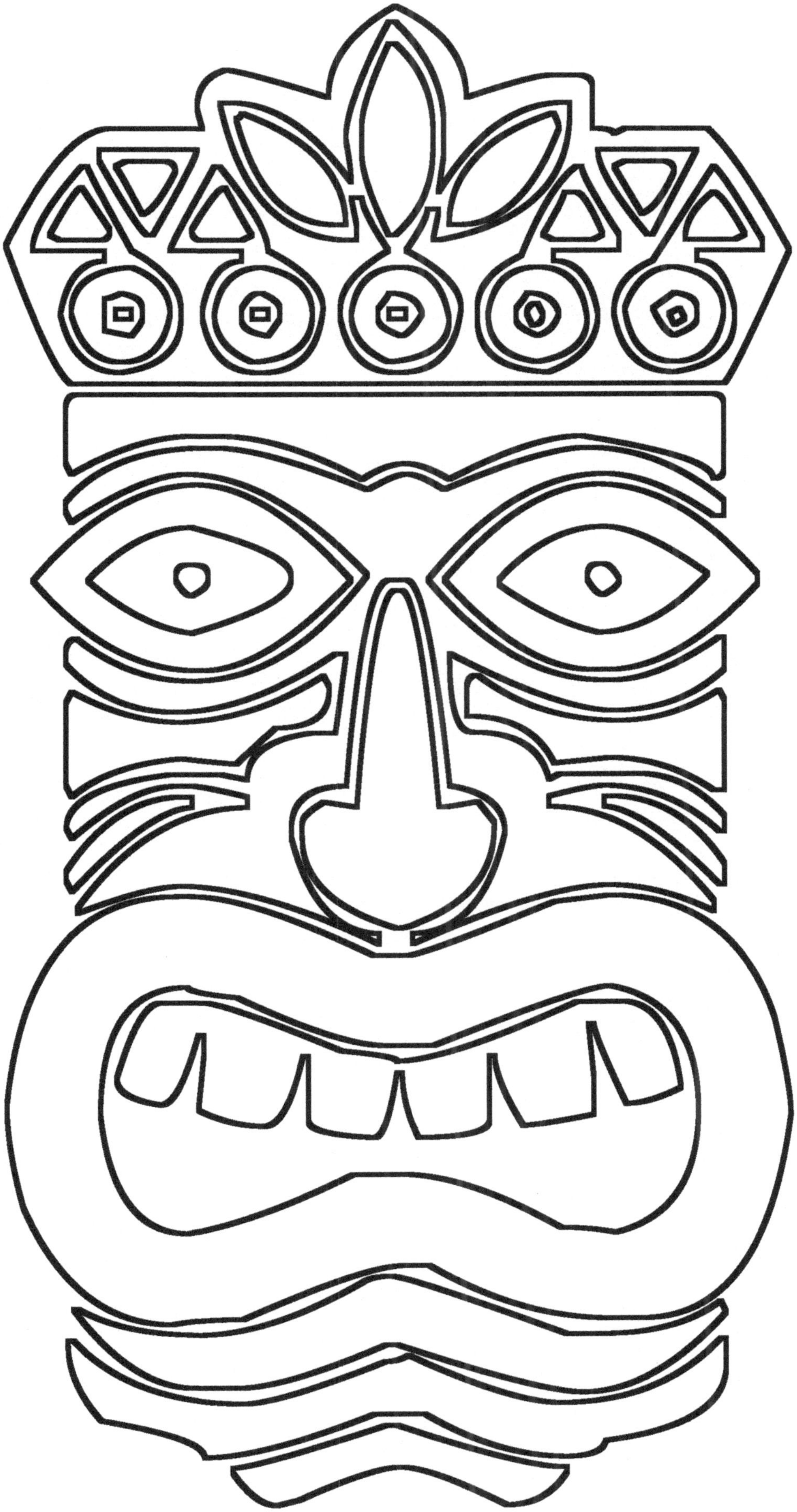

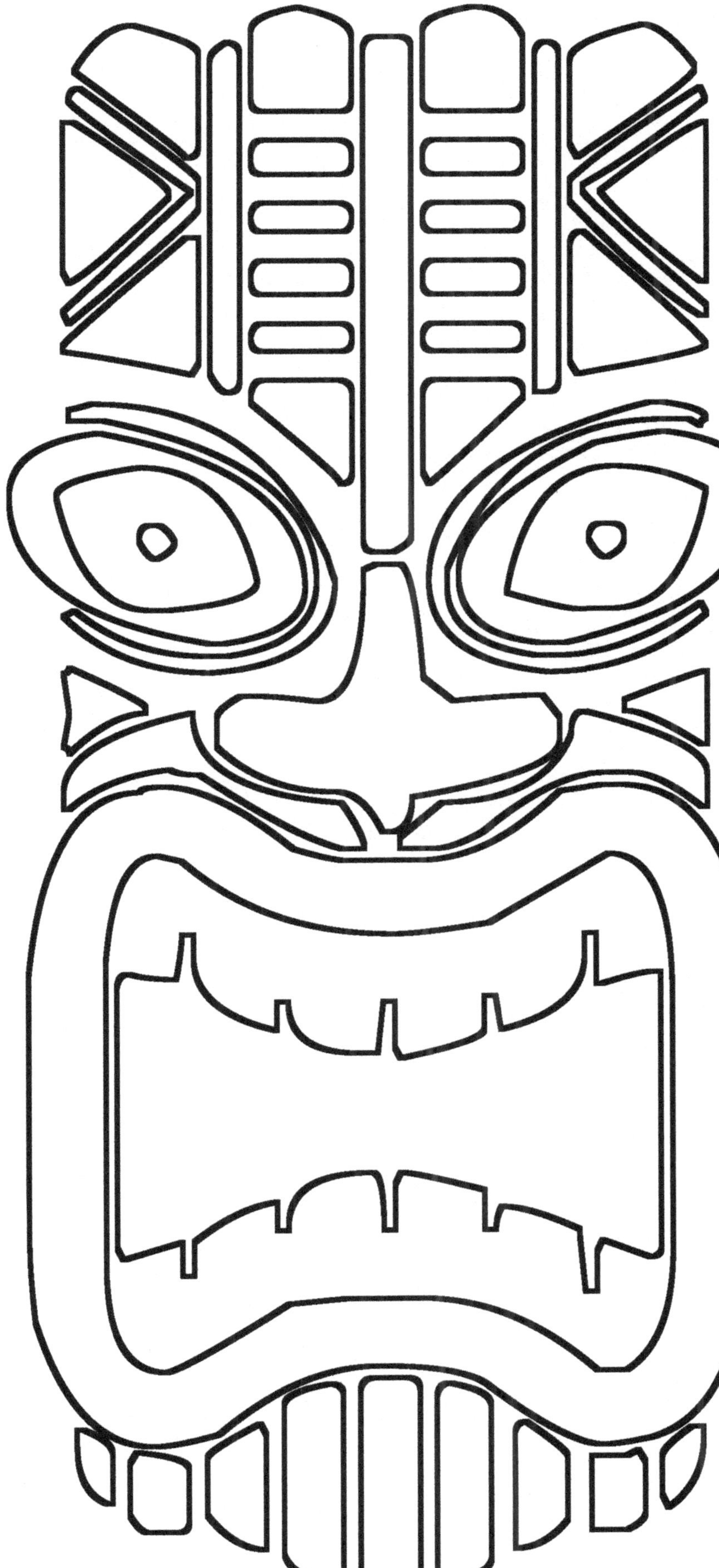

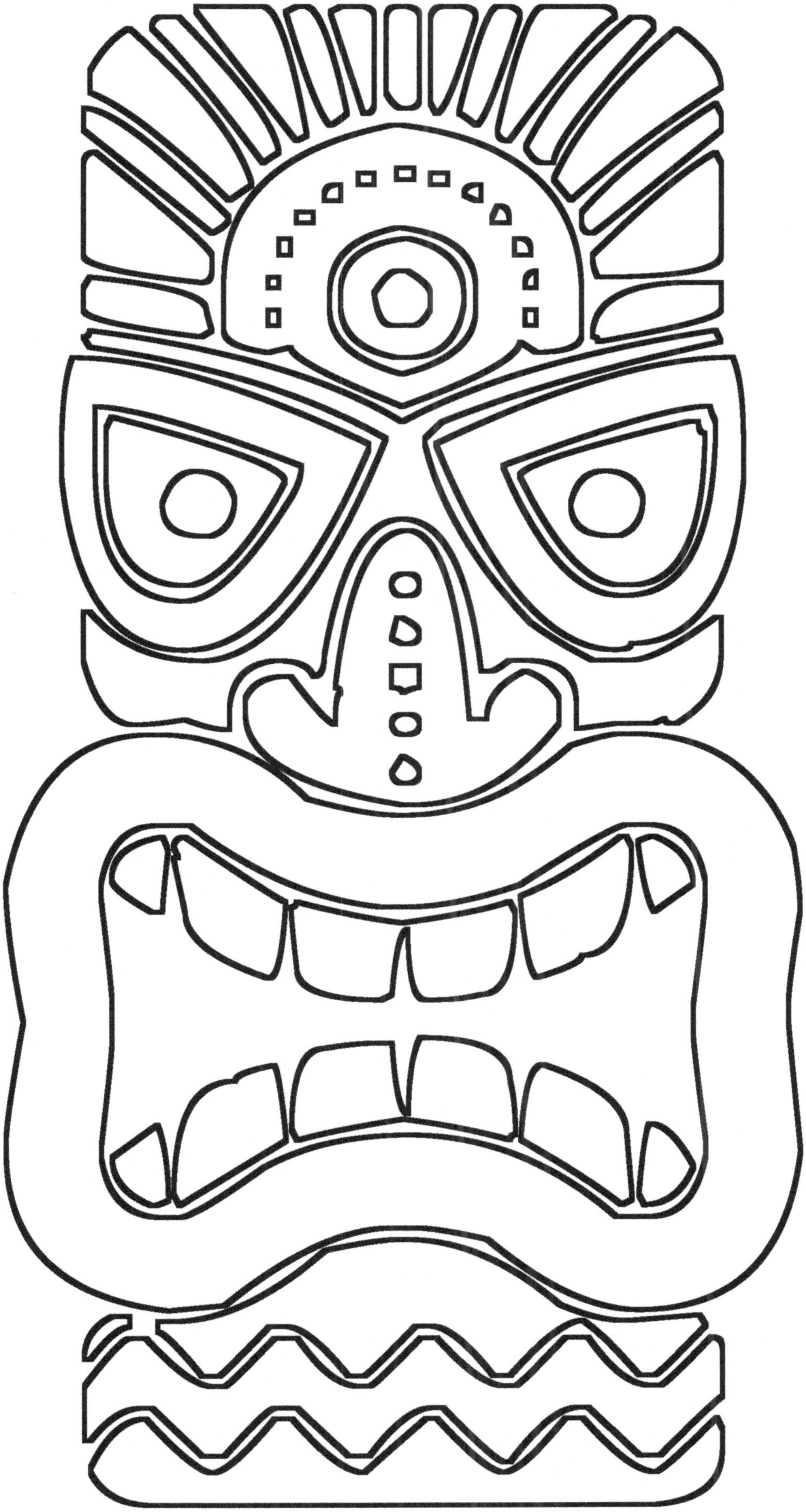

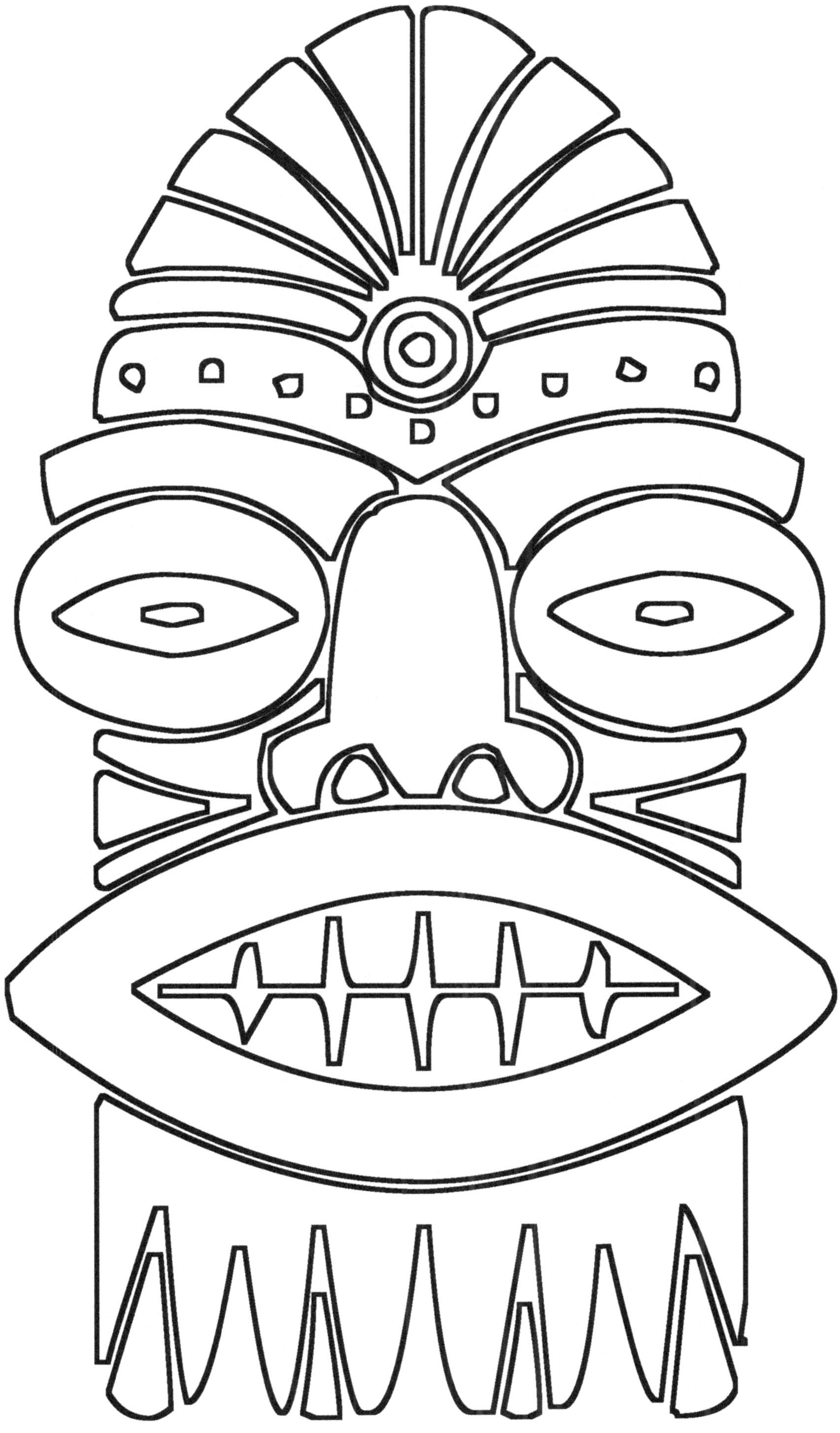

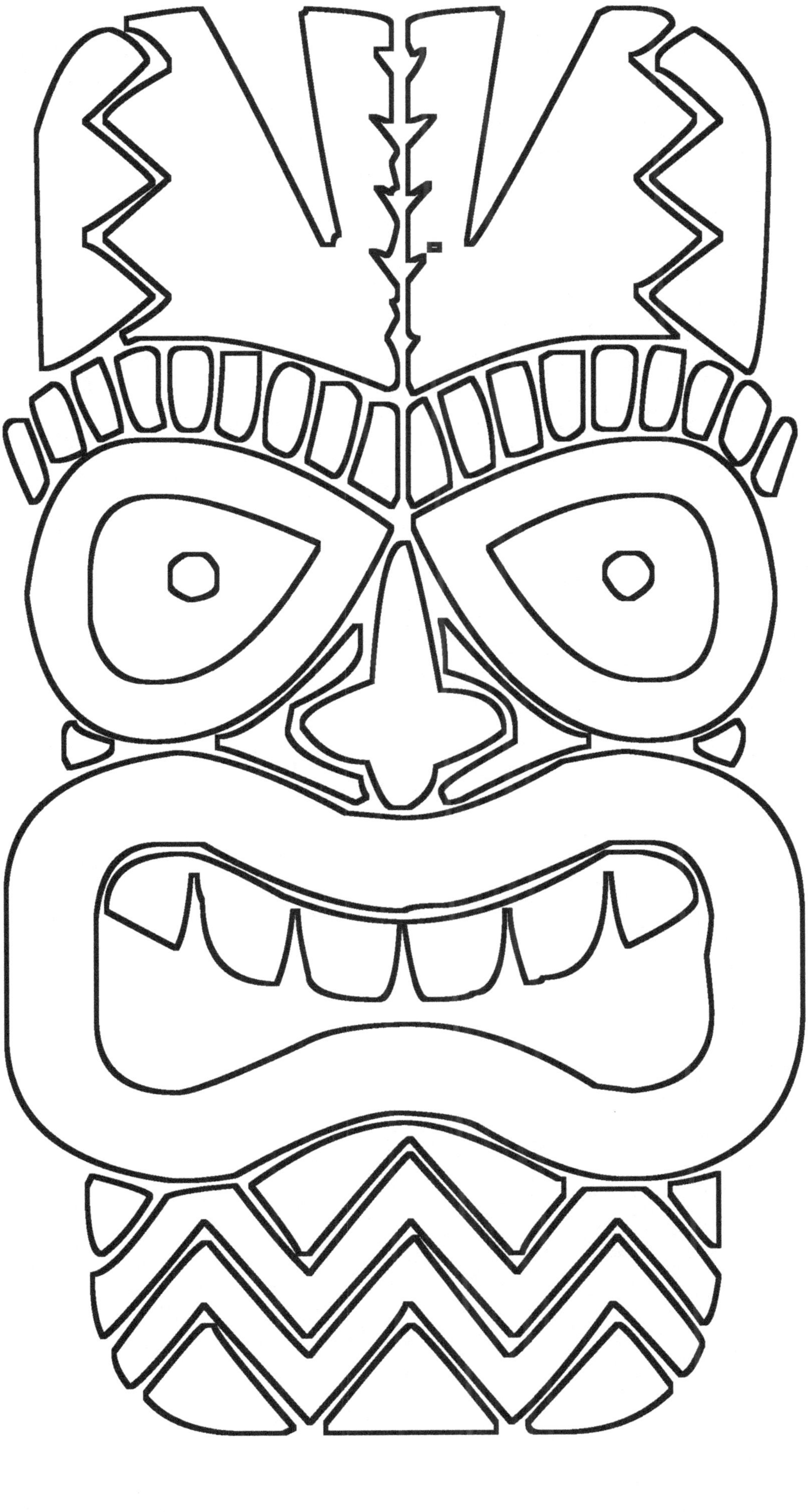

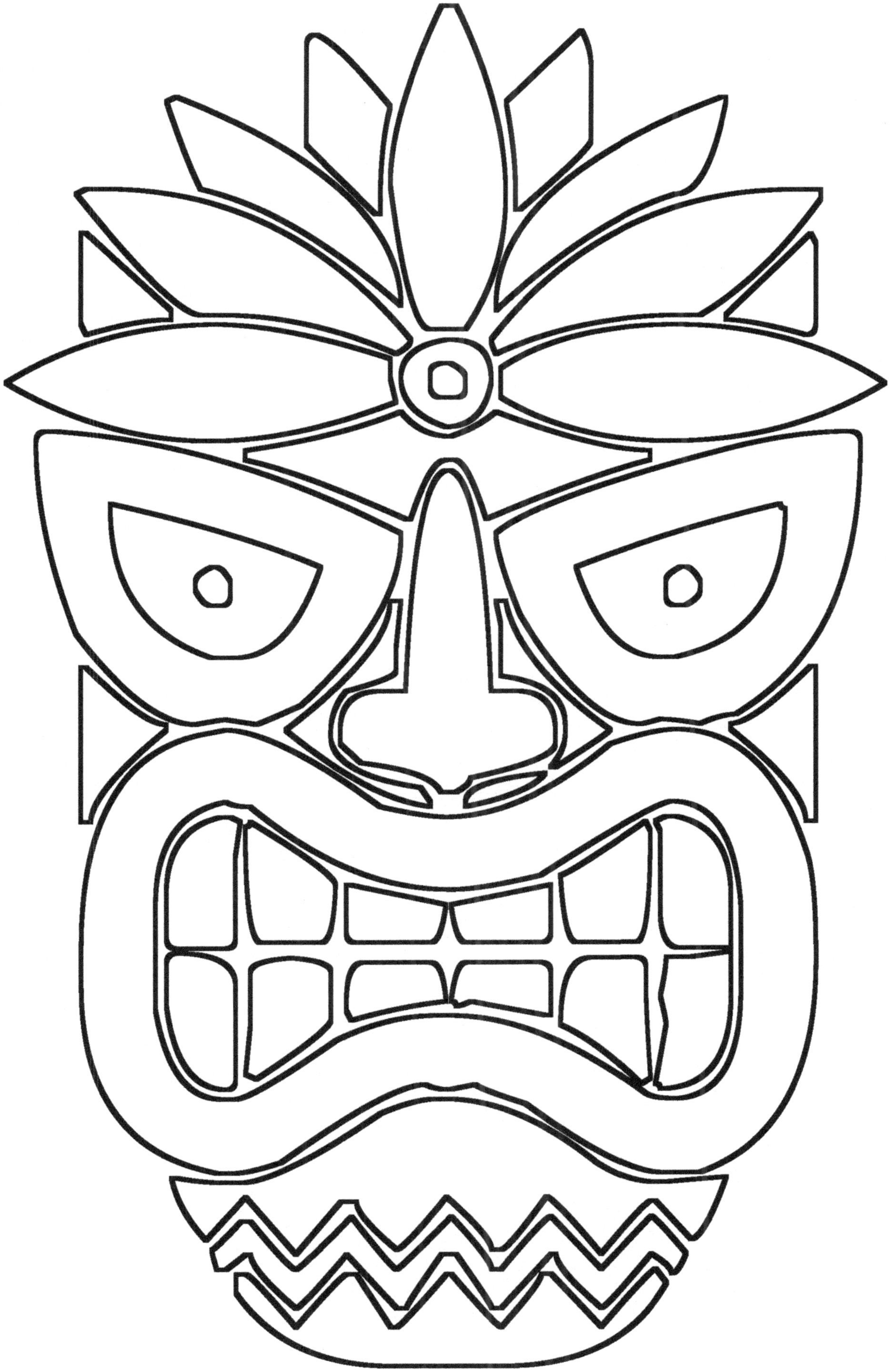

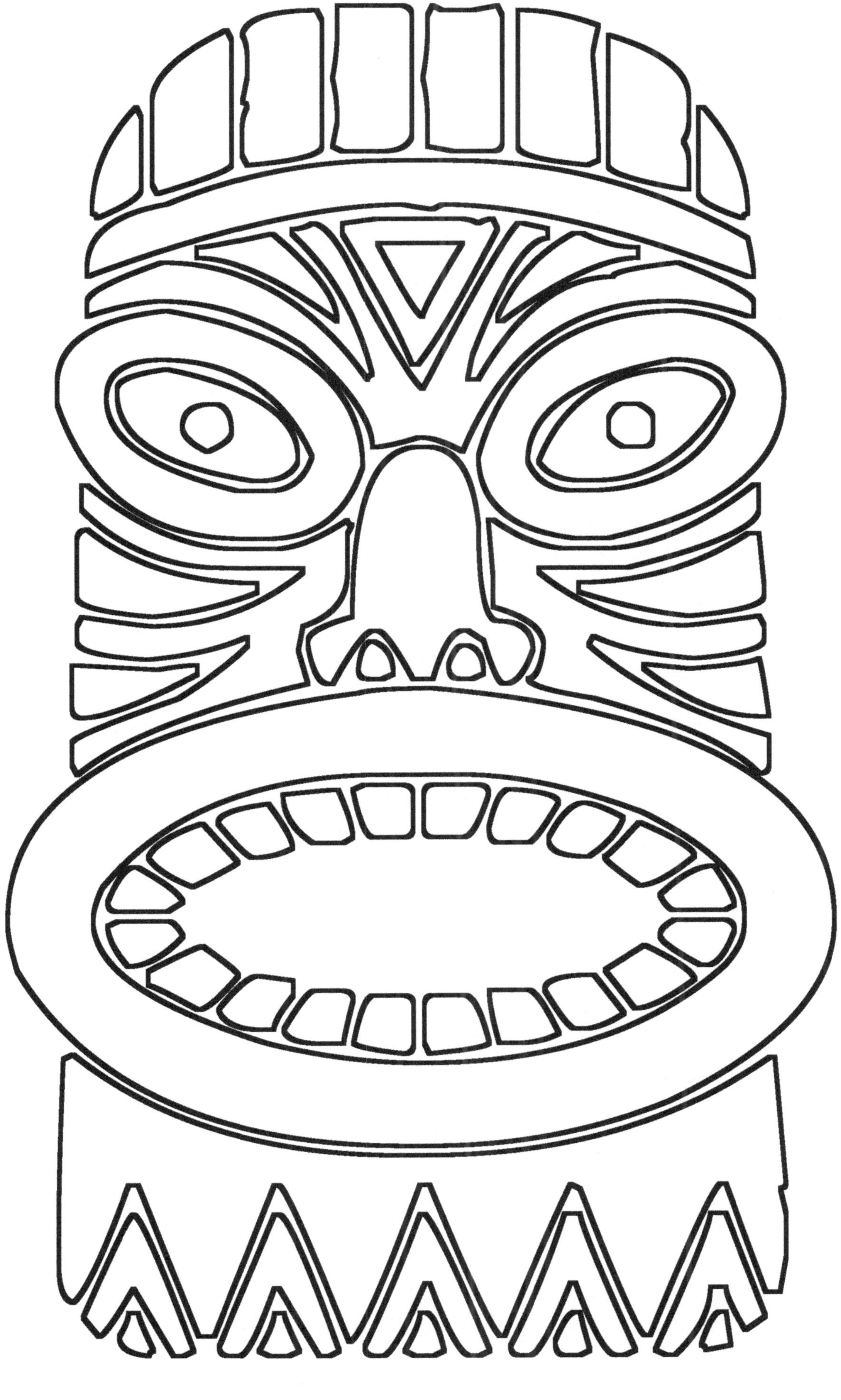

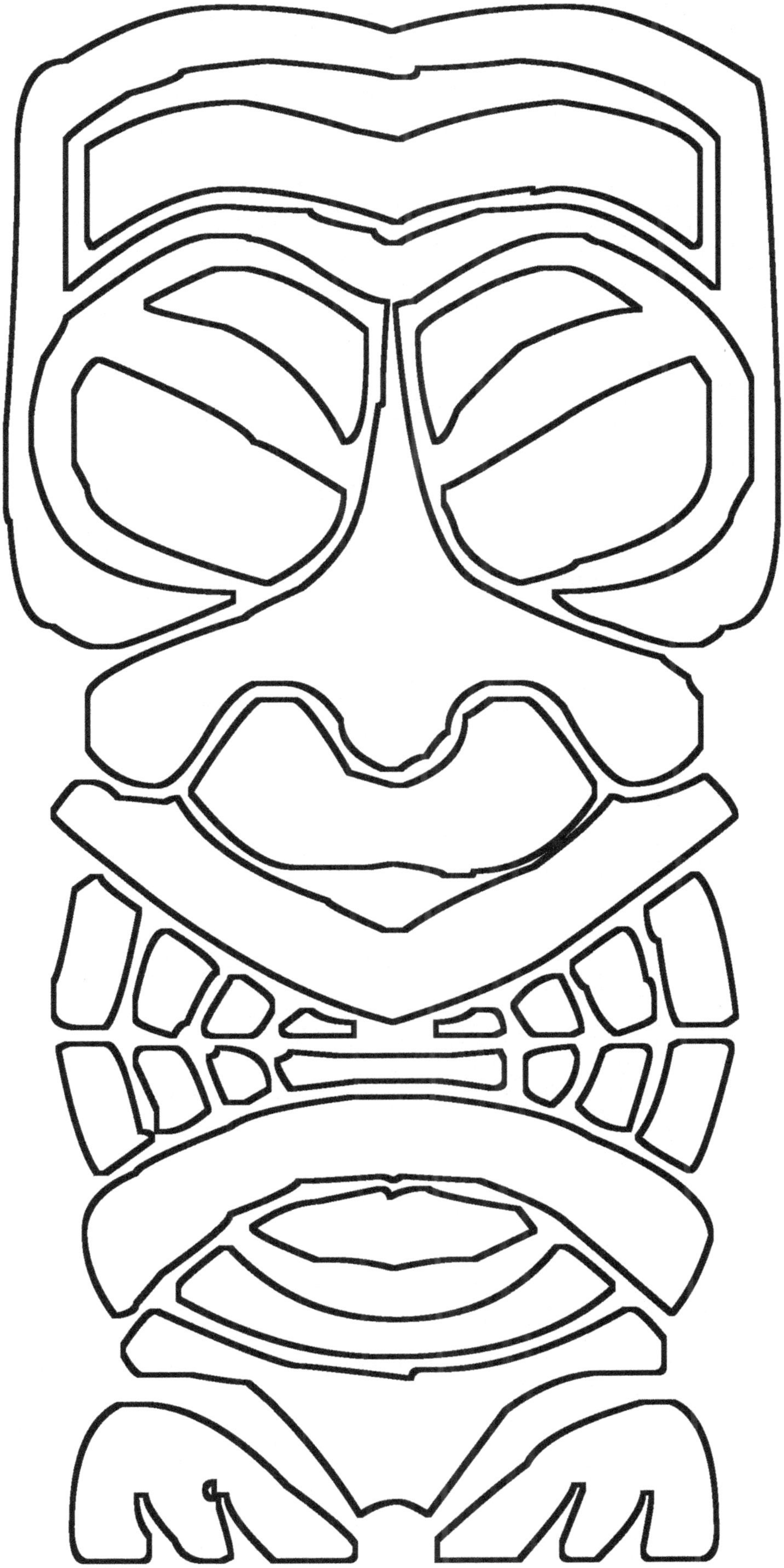

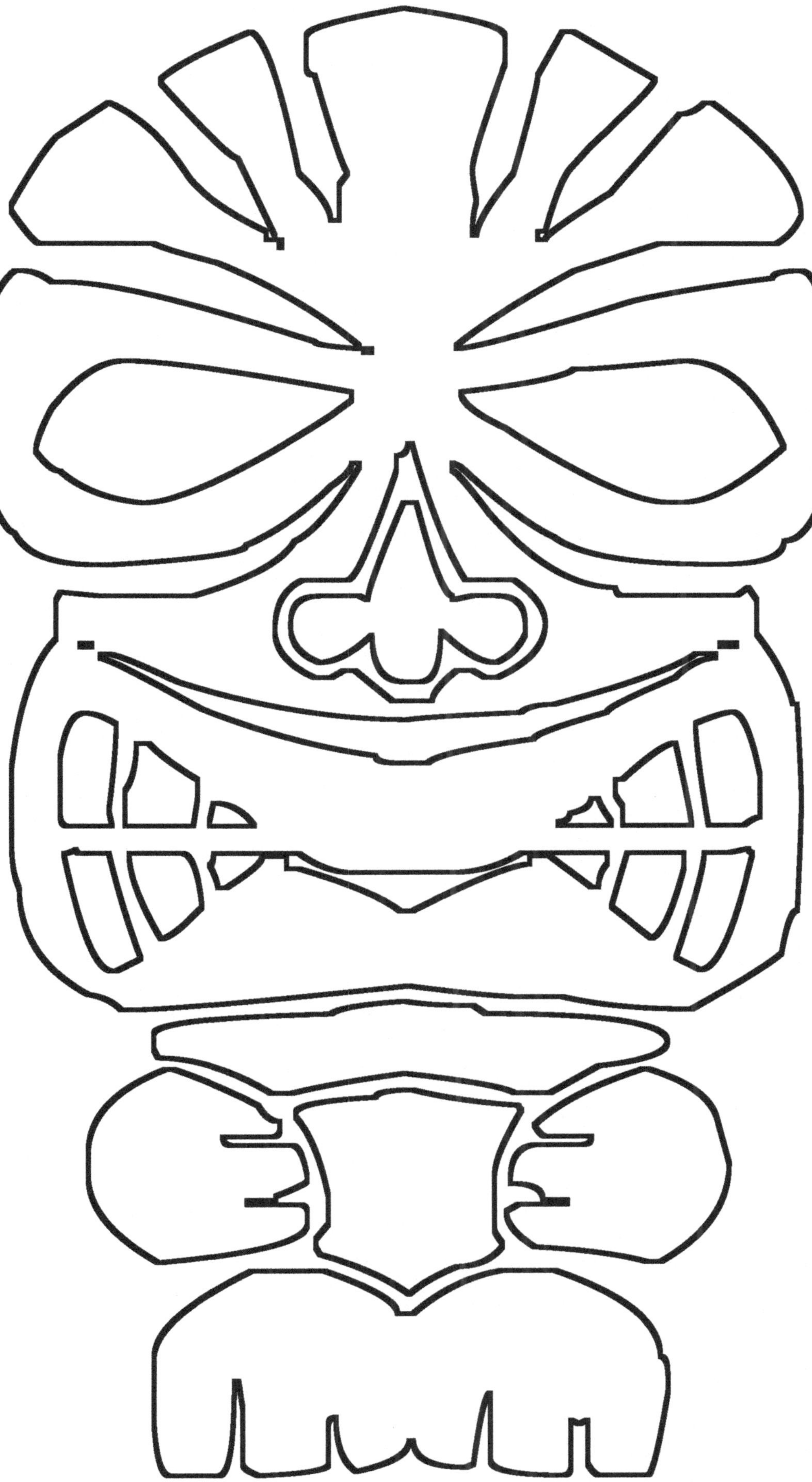

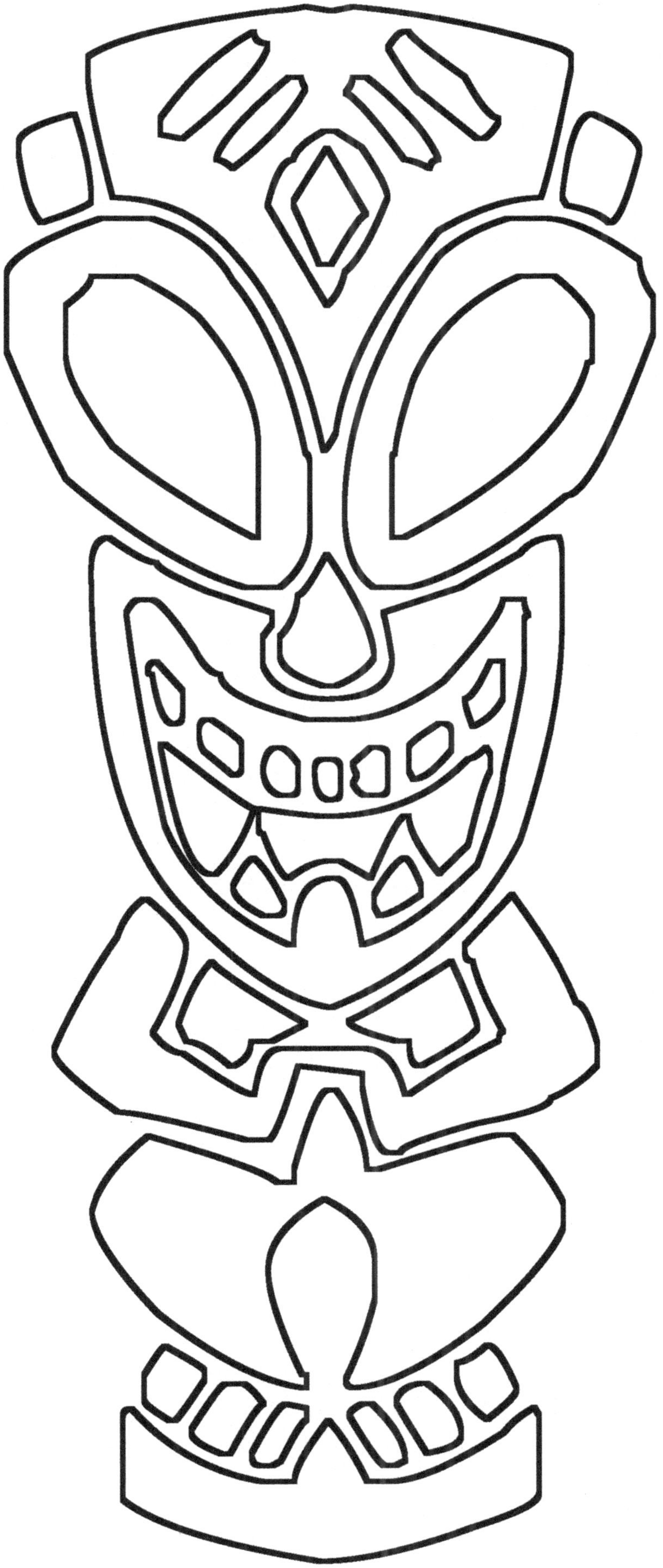

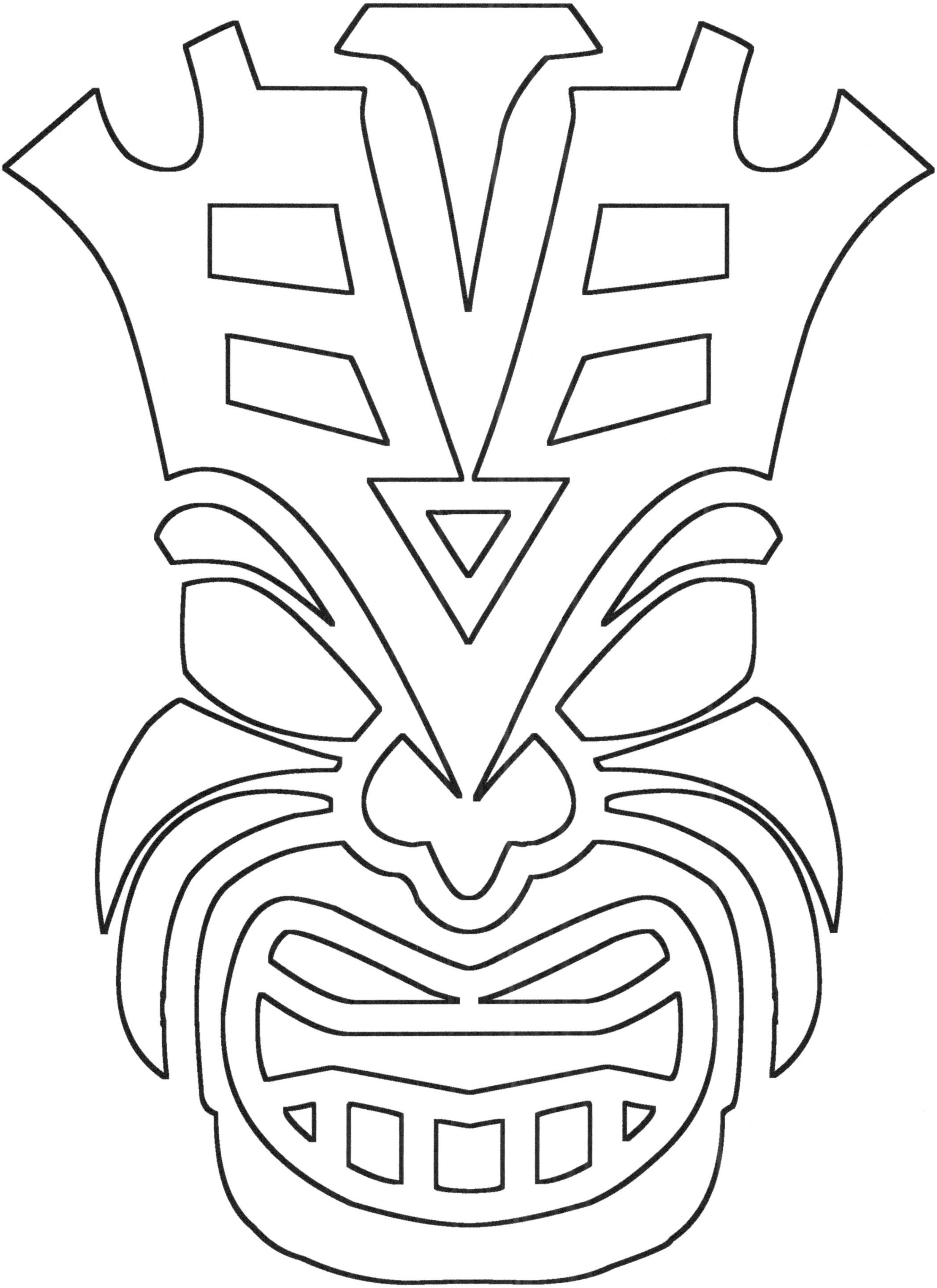

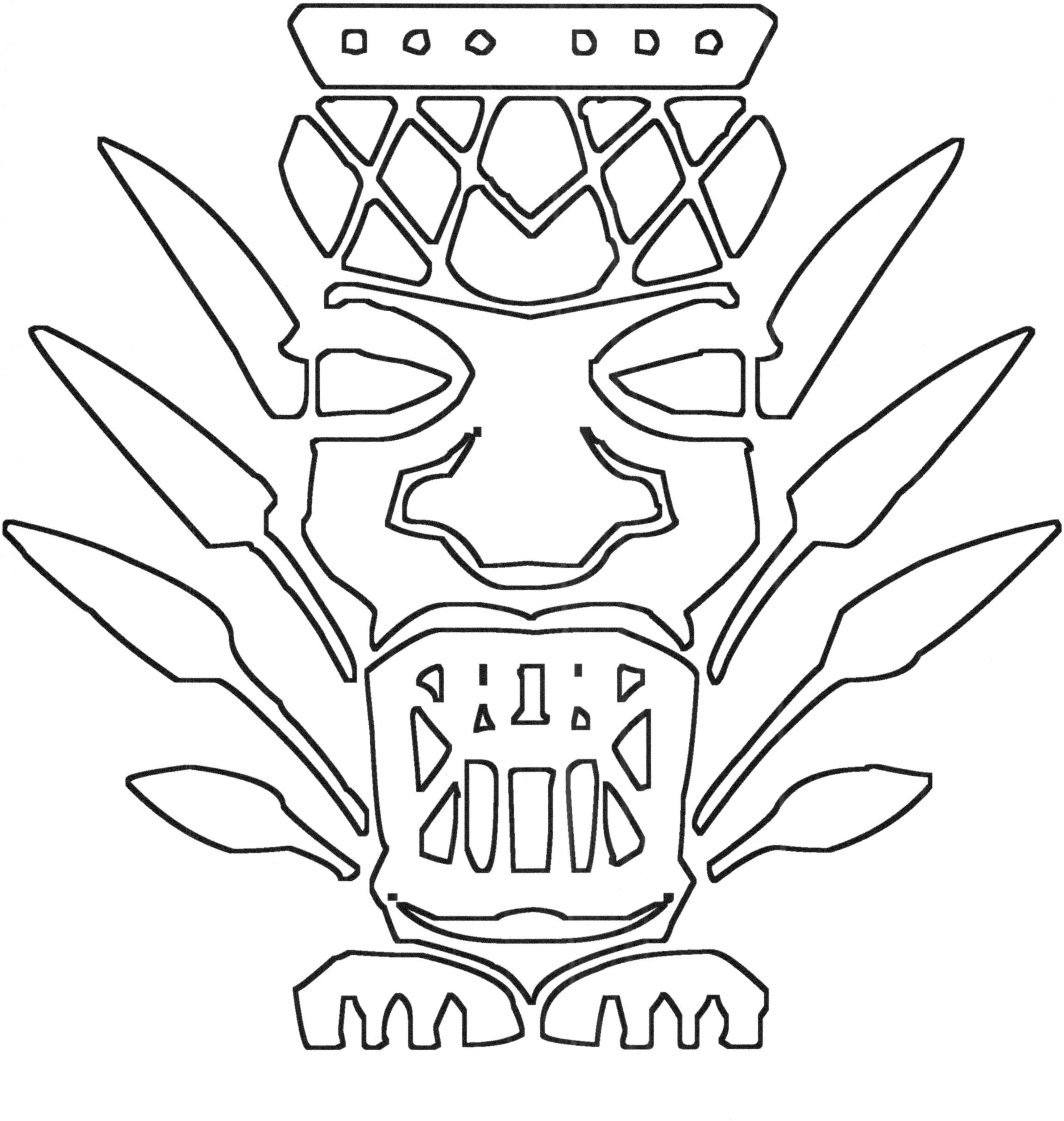

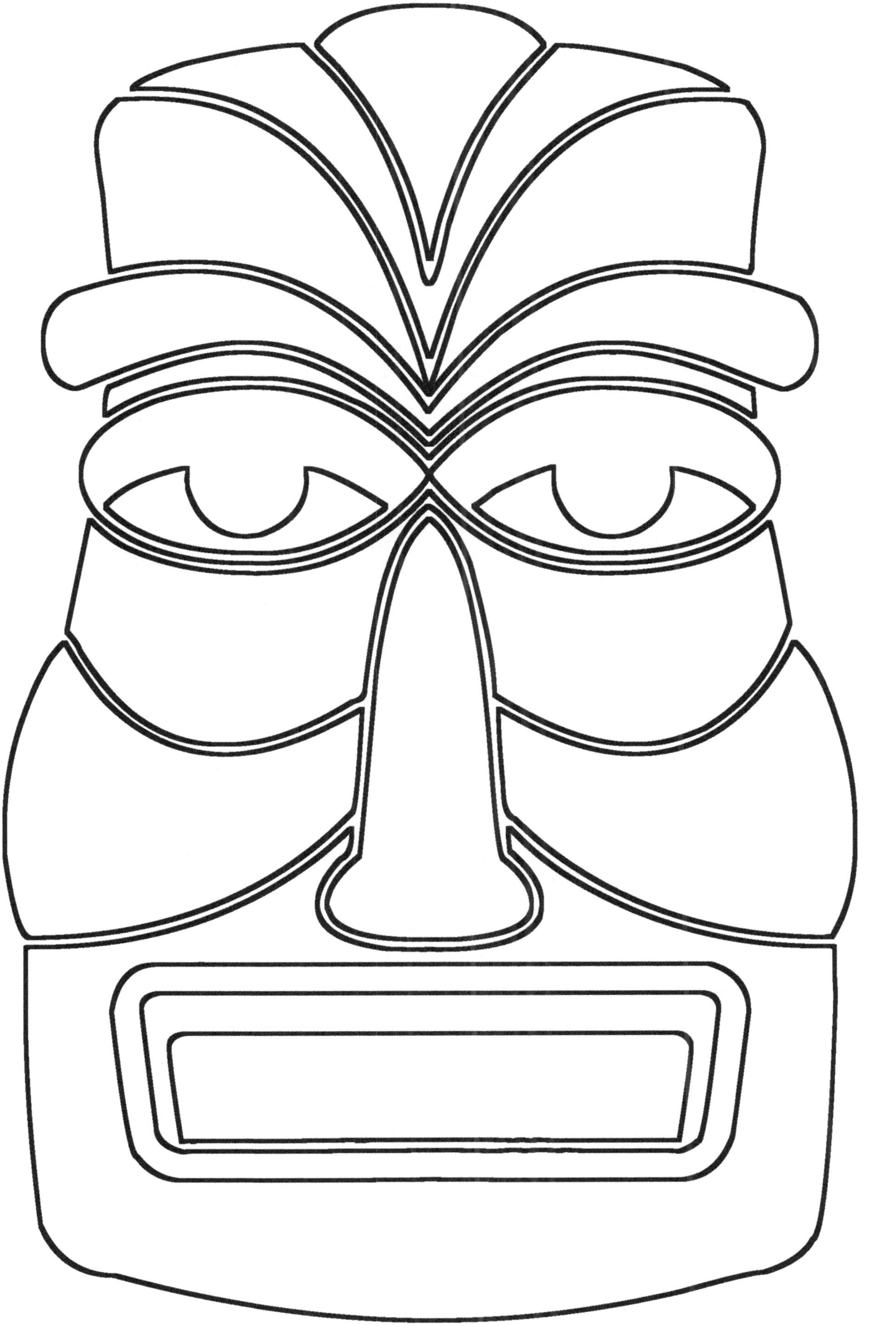

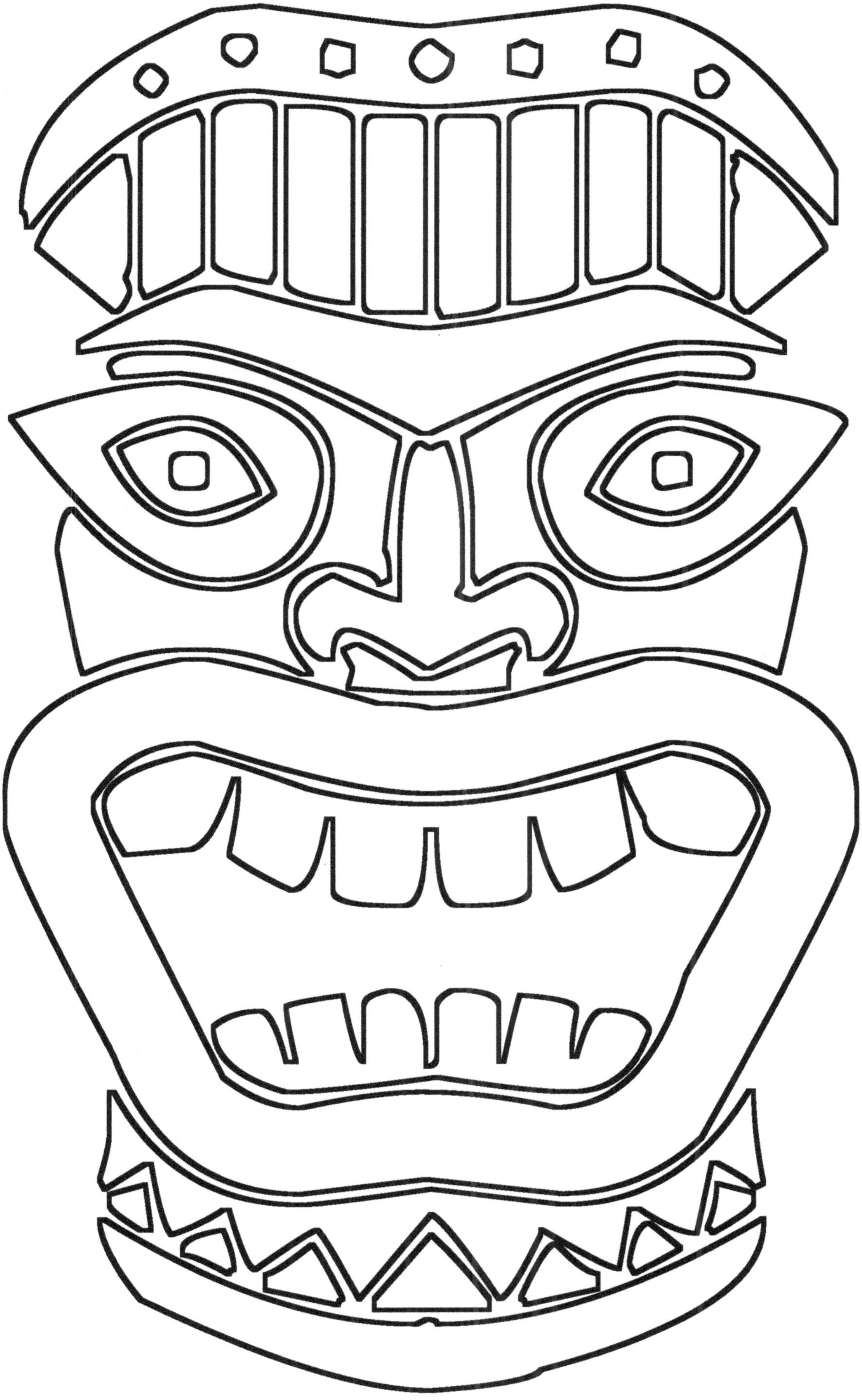

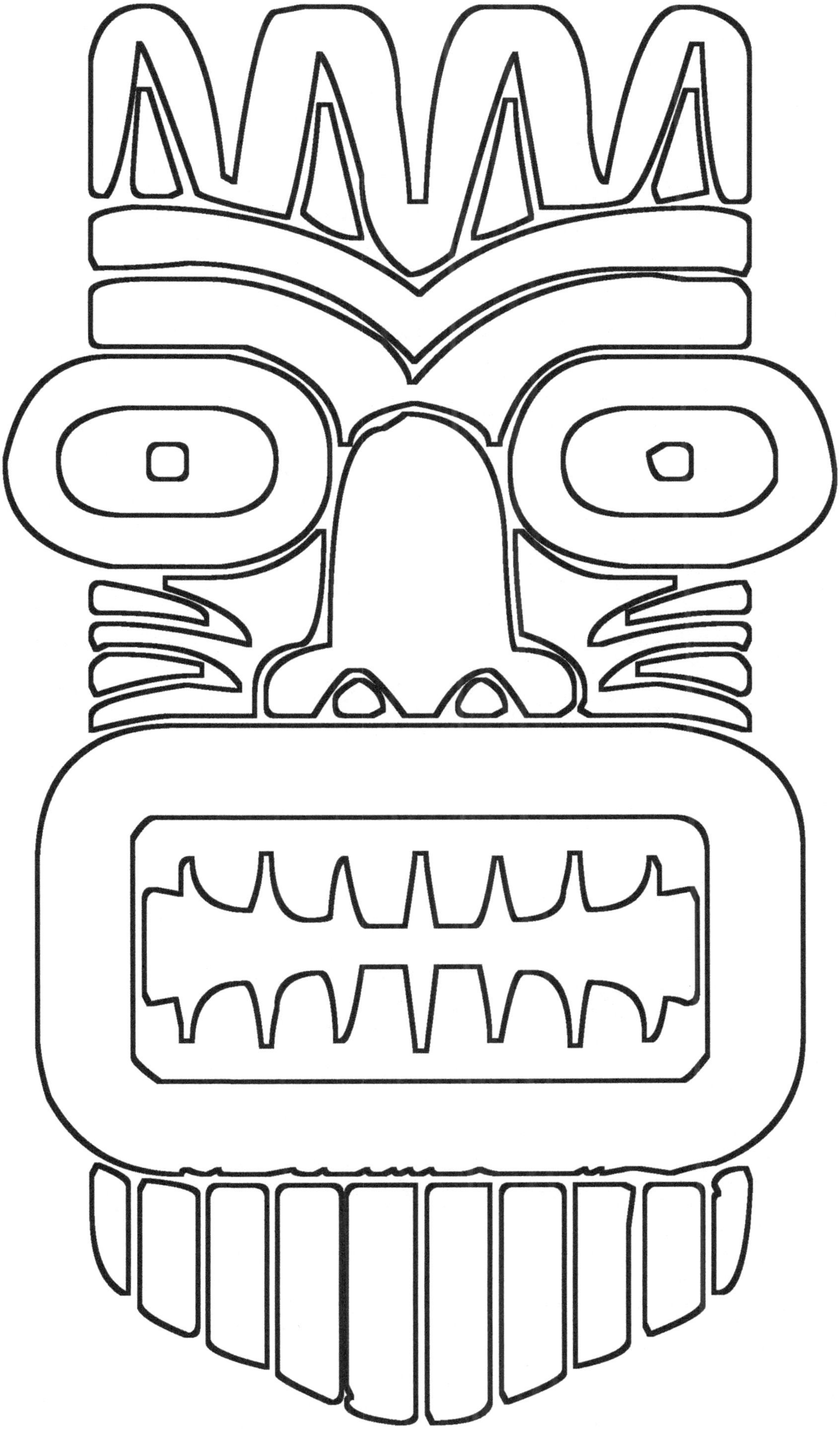

Made in the USA
Las Vegas, NV
23 December 2021

39285931R00024